Little Stars

Little Stars
BASEBALL

A CRABTREE SEEDLINGS BOOK

Taylor Farley

CRABTREE
PUBLISHING COMPANY
WWW.CRABTREEBOOKS.COM

Let's play baseball!

HENRY #91

3

We need two **teams**.

5

It's your turn to bat.

The catcher is ready with a **mitt** and a helmet.

The pitcher throws
the ball.

Be careful!
If you get three **strikes**
you are out!

You hit the ball hard.

A player in the **outfield** tries to catch it.

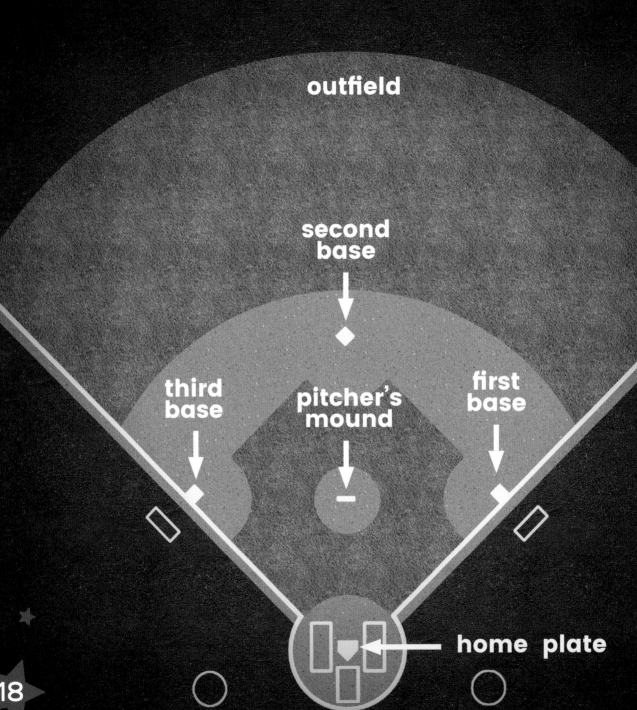

outfield

second base

third base

pitcher's mound

first base

home plate

18

Quick! Run around the **bases** to home plate!

You scored a **home run**!

20

Glossary

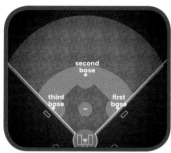

bases (BAYS-ez): There are three bases on a baseball field. They are first base, second base, and third base.

home run (HOME RUN): A batter scores a home run if he is able to run around all three bases to home plate with one hit.

mitt (MIT): A mitt is a type of baseball glove made of padded leather.

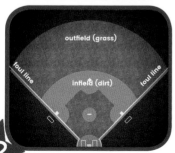

outfield (OUT-feeld): The outfield is the area beyond the infield and inside of the foul lines.

strikes (STRIKES): Strikes are throws from the pitcher that the batter swings at and misses.

teams (TEEMZ): Teams are groups of people playing a sport together on the same side.

Index

School-to-Home Support for Caregivers and Teachers

Crabtree Seedlings books help children grow by letting them practice reading. Here are a few guiding questions to help the reader build his or her comprehension skills. Possible answers are included.

Before Reading

- **What do I think this book is about?** I think this book is about playing baseball. It might teach us the rules of baseball.

- **What do I want to learn about this topic?** I want to learn about the different baseball positions.

During Reading

- **I wonder why...** I wonder why the batter is wearing a helmet.

- **What have I learned so far?** I learned that there are batters, catchers, pitchers, and players in the outfield.

After Reading

- **What details did I learn about this topic?** I learned the parts of a baseball field. There is the home plate, first base, second base, third base, the pitcher's mound, and the outfield. The bases are shaped like a diamond.

- **Write down unfamiliar words and ask questions to help understand their meaning.** I see the word *teams* on page 5 and the word *strikes* on page 12. The other vocabulary words are listed on pages 22 and 23.

Library and Archives Canada Cataloguing in Publication

Title: Little stars baseball / Taylor Farley.
Other titles: Baseball
Names: Farley, Taylor, author.
Description: Series statement: Little stars | "A Crabtree seedlings book". | Includes index. |
  Previously published in electronic format by Blue Door Education in 2020.
Identifiers: Canadiana 20200378864 | ISBN 9781427129741 (hardcover) | ISBN 9781427129925 (softcover)
Subjects: LCSH: Baseball—Juvenile literature.
Classification: LCC GV867.5 .F37 2021 | DDC j796.357—dc23

Library of Congress Cataloging-in-Publication Data

Names: Farley, Taylor, author.
Title: Little stars baseball / Taylor Farley.
Other titles: Baseball
Description: New York, NY : Crabtree Publishing Company, [2021] | Series: Little stars: a Crabtree seedlings book | Includes index.
Identifiers: LCCN 2020049385 | ISBN 9781427129741 (hardcover) | ISBN 9781427129925 (paperback)
Subjects: LCSH: Baseball--Juvenile literature.
Classification: LCC GV867.5 .F35 2021 | DDC 796.357--dc23
LC record available at https://lccn.loc.gov/2020049385

Crabtree Publishing Company
www.crabtreebooks.com   1–800–387–7650

Written by Taylor Farley
Production coordinator and Prepress technician: Samara Parent
Print coordinator: Katherine Berti

e-book ISBN 978-0-997240-16-0

Print book version produced jointly with Blue Door Education in 2021

Printed in the U.S.A./012021/CG20201102

Photo credits: Cover and page 14 © rmanera - istockphoto; pages 2-3, 4-5 © Joseph Sohm - shutterstock; pages 6-7 © Andrew Rich - istockphoto; pages 8-9 © Rob Friedman - istockphoto; pages10 and 16-17 © tammykayphoto - shutterstock; page 13 © Skip ODonnell - istockphoto; page 18 © Antony McAulay - shutterstock; page 21 © Ben Conlan - istockphoto

Published in Canada
Crabtree Publishing
616 Welland Ave.
St. Catharines, Ontario
L2M 5V6

Published in the United States
Crabtree Publishing
347 Fifth Ave.
Suite 1402-145
New York, NY 10016

Published in the United Kingdom
Crabtree Publishing
Maritime House
Basin Road North, Hove
BN41 1WR

Published in Australia
Crabtree Publishing
Unit 3 – 5 Currumbin Court
Capalaba
QLD 4157